WWHW

(WHY, WHAT, HOW-TO, WHAT-IF)

EASILY CREATE A BOOK, PODCAST, OR ONLINE COURSE IN JUST A FEW EASY-TO-FOLLOW STEPS

ROBERT PLANK

WWHW:

(Why, What, How-To, What-If)

Easily Create a Book, Podcast, or Online Course In Just a Few Easy-to-Follow Steps

By Robert Plank

Claim Your Bonus Materials: www.WWHWBook.com/gift

© 2019 by JumpX LLC, (408) 277-0904

Free Gift

If you could benefit from extra videos and guides to help you along with the process of:

- getting clear on your message
- becoming more productive
- finishing your book
- creating your podcast
- getting out of your own way
- overcoming overwhelm and survival mode

Then please accept my free gift for you here:

WWHWBook.com/gift

What People Say About This Book

"Full of awesome tips for just about everyone!

A fun read, full of stories and great information for speakers, podcasters, bloggers, authors and more.

I'm a writer and speaker - have been for years. Not only did I learn a lot, I was inspired and motivated to do some new things - a 90 minute read that has re-energized me!"

-- Chuck Hooper, Turlock, California, USA

"If you are involved in any kind of online business, this book is literally filled with Golden Nuggets of knowledge. Robert Plank is one of the most knowledgeable and plain-spoken digital entrepreneurs around.

This book contains valuable insights on not just what to do, but also covers all the things most Gurus leave out.

Having the complete picture plus helpful hints to help you get back on track if things go sideways is priceless. Highly recommended reading if you run a digital business."

-- Stephen F. Brown, Tucson, Arizona, USA

WWHW Cheatsheet

WHY should I pay attention to you, what problem are you solving for me?

- "Are you still _____?"

- Start with a "weird" emotional question or statement

- Mindset shift

WHAT principles do you want me to know, and what problem are we solving together?

- "Imagine..."

- What's in it for me?

- What alternatives don't work? (no, old, new, right)

HOW do I solve this problem and what are the steps?

- "Let's Do It..."

- What steps are we about to take? Show me each step. What steps did we just take?

- What is your system? "Introducing..."

WHAT-IF I solve this problem by taking action now? What new possibilities open up to me?

- Question, assignment, challenge, or checklist

- Sell me on the idea

- "Go Ahead, Do It Right Now."

Preface: Not Everyone Thinks Like You

Place one penny and one nickel on a table in front of you.
What do you see?

You might see one small coin and one larger coin. One is
worth 5 cents and another worth 1 cent. Someone else could
see copper vs. nickel. Or brown vs. silver. The nickel is
thicker than the penny. You could compare weight. One
personality vs. another might focus on the similarities
between those two coins, or the differences.

Were you ever taught in grade school that some people are
visual learners, others learn auditorily, and others
kinesthetically, through touching and doing? I thought it
was cheesy advice, until years later, through high school and
college, I found myself speaking more quickly than others.

Speaking quickly does not mean you are smart. Speaking slowly does NOT mean you are dumb! It means that you're different, but what most of the population is unaware of is this: when you speak differently than someone else, they'll think you're unintelligent. When you speak LIKE them, they'll think you're intelligent.

It cannot be helped! It is tribalism. If you're more visual, then you'll speak more quickly, since "sight" information is expressed quicker than "hearing." Listen to an "auditory" learner speak, and you'll think to yourself: that person is an idiot. Can't they get the words out faster? But then, when that "auditory" person hears you, a "visual" person, speak (in this example), they're thinking to themselves: that visual person is an idiot! They're babbling. Their words are spewing out at a mile a minute. Can't they slow down, take their time, and let the words sink in?

It is possible to be energetic and appear intelligent, but also make sense, be calm, be entertaining, and communicate in accessible language. It's also important to get over speaking butterflies, inward thinking, writer's block, and the rest, to focus on helping OTHERS. If you're speaking with someone one-on-one (as I do with podcast interviews), match the other person's speed, language, and metaphors, to meet them where they're at.

Here's a fun question that I hope you'll answer for me: **are you a square, triangle, circle, or squiggle?**

For some reason, you are drawn to one of the above figures. One simply jumps out at you, it's just THE one! Here's a quick test you can take yourself -- and have others take as well:

First take a blank piece of paper, and draw each of the above symbols with a pen or marker. Draw the square, triangle, circle, and squiggle on the top half of the sheet of paper. It's important that you use pen and paper for this so you can see the symbols in front of you, hear the sound your pen makes as you draw it, and feel what it's like to draw each symbol.

Next, choose your favorite symbol and draw that same symbol TWICE on the bottom half of that sheet of paper. It must be the same symbol. You might choose to draw a circle twice, or two squiggles, or a triangle and another triangle.

You're left with a sheet of paper like this: on the top half, you've drawn a square, triangle, circle, and squiggle. On the bottom half: two squares. Or two triangles, or two circles, or two squiggles. What does it mean?

You are multiple people -- the person you think you are, the person you are, the person you want to be, and the person others see. Here's what your "results" say about you:

- If you're a **CIRCLE**, then you're a listener and problem solver. You focus on the *WHY*.

- If you're a **SQUARE**, then you're an organizer and perfectionist. You focus on the *WHAT*.

- If you're a **TRIANGLE**, then you're a leader/decider and the *HOW-TO* is most important to you.

- If you're a **SQUIGGLE**, then you're a creative (inventor) type who is most concerned about the possibilities or the *WHAT-IF*.

What can you do with this? **One:** associate with others who think differently than you. If you're a circle, partner with a square. If you're a squiggle, have a triangle on your team.

Two: Realize that not everyone thinks the same as you. You may be interested in "getting it done" -- others may be interested in the reason it's important, or the possibilities that are available once it's done.

Three: When teaching anything, speak to the **Why's**, then the **What's**, then **How-To's**, then the **What-If** people. This way, you'll include everyone at some point AND you'll take people on an exciting start-to-finish journey when telling a story or teaching information.

Introduction: Questions & Formulas

It's your choice: Stress, unhappiness, regret.

Or: Happiness, fulfillment, success.

Which do you want?

I realize how easy it is to fall into "head trash" thinking and let stress get the better of you. You've considered giving up. Letting writer's block "win." Others seem to have it so easy!

And yet, I'm sure that in your travels you've met at least one person who didn't have much (tangible, material-wise) and was not only happy, but ALSO fulfilled. There are also those who seem to have everything, far more than you, and are completely miserable! What's the secret?

It's this: ask a powerful question and use a pre-existing template to help you with the answer. If you aren't where you want to be in life, if you make poor decisions, if you can't get out of your own way... it's because you're asking the wrong questions, or providing the wrong answers for yourself, or both.

Before diving into specifics, I want to share a concept with you that completely changed my life: **ikigai.**

Ikigai (pronounced "ee-key-guy")

This Japanese word means "a reason for being." It's the meaning of life! Money alone won't make you happy. You might have passion for a hobby that pays no money. You could have an in-demand skill but no personal love for it.

You must tick all four boxes to achieve life purpose: what you **love**, what you're **good at**, what you can be **paid for**, and what the world **needs**.

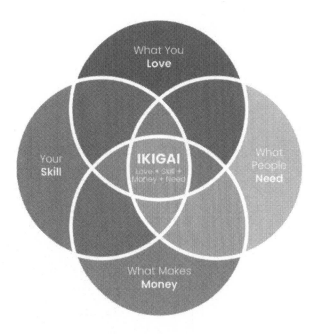

It's your job to get past the negativity, self-sabotage, over-complication and various obstacles to get your "thing" created: that book, podcast, video, or blog post. **And help others get results in the process!**

Use Questions to Make Decisions

Which is a better question to ask of yourself?

- "How can I possibly survive today?"

- Or, "What three things am I grateful to have right now?"

- "How do I pay these stupid bills?"

- Or, "What specific actions will I take today to earn money to provide for my family?"

- "Why does everything go wrong for me?"

- Or, "What is good about my current situation? What COULD be good about my current situation?"

Your mind has been trained since childhood to answer questions. You can use questions to work your subconscious while you sleep. Example: one night I was stuck thinking of an attention-getting headline to write for a web page I was building. Before going to bed, I wrote the following (five times) in my spiral bound notebook:

"What 25 great headlines could I write for my website?"

When I awoke the next morning, I didn't have all 25 headlines created, but I had a jumpstart on some ideas.

S.C.A.M.P.E.R. Thinking

Your brain is a computer. By asking specific questions, you can instruct it to compute any solution you want, even if that question is, "Decision A or B?" Or, "What details should I provide to the expert who will do this job for me?"

When things need to change, think S.C.A.M.P.E.R. -- coined by Bob Eberle:

- **Substitute:** What can I remove or replace in this situation?

- **Combine:** Can two or more of these elements be merged?

- **Adapt:** Can this be made more flexible to provide additional functionality?

- **Modify (or Magnify or Minify):** What one attribute of this project or scenario can be changed?

- **Purpose:** How can I put this to a completely different use than was originally intended?

- **Eliminate:** What can be removed from this situation?

- **Rearrange (or Reverse):** How could you the order of steps or use the product in the exact opposite way it was ended?

Not only can the above be used for simple decision-making, I use the above elements to edit my writing. One pass to eliminate unnecessary words, another to look for possible replacements. Can this story at the beginning be moved to the end, or perhaps rearrange chapters?

I'm a computer programmer and one of my best-selling products is a website backup tool called Backup Creator.

- I frequently *Substitute* different sub-components of the backup process to make it work more smoothly.

- I've *Combined* steps so that the end-user only has to click a button to backup or restore their website.

- We were able to *Adapt* the plugin to copy a website to a new location in addition to simple backup/restore.

- Our team also *Modified* the plugin so that if a backup is sent offsite to cloud storage, it can delete the local backup to save space.

- In the future, we may find a new *Purpose* for our backup functionality: to offload (basically, auto-backup) a website's files to the cloud to decrease storage costs and decrease website load time.

- I am constantly looking to *Eliminate* the extra time our software takes to create a backup, and create smaller backups by not backing up all the junk... backups from other tools, spam comments, temporary files.

- An interesting spin on our backup plugin came from thinking about *Reversal*. A backup plugin allows you to create a library of multiple website backups. The reverse of that setup would be a library of pre-made templates people could use to create already-made sites. I have also "Rearranged" the steps in the backup process to make it function better.

Enough technical talk! The point is: when you're searching for outside-the-box solutions, think S.C.A.M.P.E.R.

S.M.A.R.T. Goals

Since that formula takes care of your minor scrapes and jams, let's focus on the bigger picture: your goals. What are you trying to accomplish, complete, or build? Many people fall short of their goals, aren't excited enough, or even self-sabotage because their goals are not compelling. They aren't asking the right questions, and they fail to structure their goals in the proper way.

- **Dieting goals:** typically too complex and ambitious (I'll run 5 miles a day and lift weights daily, but don't stick to it)

- **Financial goals:** no consistent tracking in place (I want to get out of debt but continue with poor day-to-day spending habits)

- **Relationship goals:** no plan or daily actions (I want a happier marriage, but I haven't taken any steps to make it a reality)

- **Knowledge goals:** too vague (I want to go back to school, but I haven't decided where I'd attend, or what degree I would complete)

- **Business or career goals:** no deadline (I want to grow my business, but I have no sense of urgency about it)

Don't underestimate the importance of setting proper goals. Think about how many people who try fad diets, only to gain more weight than they lost in the end. Or how many people buy a bottle of vitamins, yet those supplements expire before they're put to use? How many people buy a book without finishing?

What you're missing in the equation: create S.M.A.R.T. goals. This is an acronym that stands for:

- **Specific:** something tangible (so you know when you've hit your target), and simple enough to be explained in one single sentence (so you can keep it in your head and easily explain it to others without drawing out a huge spider-web diagram)

- **Measurable:** traceable progress (metrics)

- **Action-Oriented:** things you can do that are within your control

- **Relevant:** a goal that relates to your life plan

- **Time-Bound:** a deadline by which point you plan to reach this goal

Anytime you set a goal for yourself, ensure that it is specific, measurable, actionable, relevant, and time-bound — to ensure it becomes something you complete, and feel good about! As they say, "Nothing diminishes anxiety faster than action."

When you're acting instead of reacting, being strategic, and taking real steps towards where you want to go, you'll find that you overthink less and accomplish more. As they also say, "If you want something done, ask a busy person." Objects in motion tend to stay in motion. If you're unsatisfied or bored, perhaps you aren't setting goals that excite you. If you feel "burned out" then you aren't setting stretch goals that challenge you.

The secret to making decisions is to ask questions and use templates to work on the answers. To think outside the box, S.C.A.M.P.E.R. by Substituting, Combining, Adapting, Modifying, Purposing, and Eliminating. And ensure you are setting S.M.A.R.T. goals which are Specific, Measurable, Action-Oriented, Relevant, and Time-Bound.

The most important formula you'll use when expressing yourself, conquering writer's block, presenting information on webinars, and overall, communicating more effectively, is **W.W.H.W. — Why, What, How-To, What-If.**

Chapter 1: Why, What, How-To, What-If

(The Templated Structure That Obliterates Writer's Block and Gets Attention Every Time)

Objective: Write (or say) something interesting, that gets noticed, makes sense, is easy to follow, is quick (and fun) for you to create, entertains, and makes an impact.

Writer's block, awkward silence, blank computer screen. Stop me if you've had this problem before at some point: **you DON'T know what to say or write!**

Maybe you need to give a presentation soon (in person, in online webinar format, as a podcast or YouTube video), but you're second guessing yourself. How do you introduce yourself? Should you jump right in to some steps? Maybe it's a report for work, or an essay for school.

Remember those cringe-worthy days, staring at a blank computer screen or blank sheet of paper? How do you begin? With a "thesis statement" that summarizes? "Webster's dictionary defines [word] as..." How boring! "The purpose of this essay is to show you..." Not compelling.

Here's the answer you're looking for:
Why, What, How-To, What-If.

"Why, What, How-To, What-If" is THE formula that ensures you create that YouTube tutorial video, document those instructions, or speak about a topic in such a way that relates to the largest number of people, AND is exciting in all the right ways, PLUS is just the right length for whatever you want to accomplish.

Have you ever been in a conversation with someone, and they immediately dumped a bunch of information on you? You feel like you missed something. Or, let's say the discussion was winding down and the person seemed to be ramping up a new line of conversation. You may be writing or presenting video instructions and your content is "off" in the same way. Perhaps you meander too much in one area, or you make your steps in the wrong order.

You can LIVE within that structured creativity and add your own uniqueness within that structure.

You ARE unique and creative, but you must use the "foundation" of a template to avoid reinventing the wheel, to give your action-taking a jumpstart and hit the ground running with your progress -- if you'll allow me to use three metaphors at once.

The Rule of Threes

Speaking of three's, here's an easy structure you'll never un-see: the rule of threes. **Pop quiz: which is a more "compelling" statement?**

A. If you'll give me just a few minutes of your time today, I'll show you how to make more money while you sleep.

B. Give me a few minutes today and I'll show you how to: make more money, get more time, AND lose weight.

C. In just a few minutes, I'll show you: how to make more money, save the money you make, get more time, lose weight, gain energy, have more fun, feel better, live longer, and be happier!

You may have been tempted to answer "C" -- but there's something wrong with that statement, isn't there? It's a laundry list. I'm overloaded. It lacks focus.

Instead of making a single statement or a long list, you'll have impact when you list three items to focus on. You'll notice the "listing three things" technique used again and again in speaking and writing.

Three Why's

Joy/sadness, anger/fear, trust/disgust, surprise/anticipation. When you're looking to communicate information or evoke change, emotions trump logic. It's important to make people feel, but you must also be concise and get to the point.

That's where the "Three Why's" technique appears. I want to say (Statement 1). But why? The reason that's important is (Statement 2). Why is that? Because of (Statement 3). That final statement will be more emotion-driven and **get to the core of what someone wants.**

Quick exercise: Tell me, why should I take my family to Disneyland this summer?

1. Why? Because there are many new attractions and the price of admission is cheap compared to what you'll experience. (logic-based argument centered on price)

2. Why? The fun adventures you have will be irreplaceable and bring you closer as a family

3. Why? Those adventures are crucial because they'll shape your children's lives forever, and you'll never get that time back. In fact, you never know how much time you have left.

Templated Structure (WWHW)

You learned the alphabet, grammar, words, sentences, and paragraphs in order to "conform." However, you can use your own "unique" written words and spoken language in order to stand out. Here's the formula that will change everything in your writing and presentations:

- **WHY** is this important in the first place?

- **WHAT** are you about to show me?

- **HOW** do I take the steps to do this?

- **WHAT-IF** I do this, what are the next steps?

I've seen a few people complicate these steps and try to "claim" they invented this structure, but it doesn't need to be any more complicated than Why, What, How-To, What-If...

It's important to apply WWHW in the proper SEQUENCE. It's not just a matter of covering your bases or applying "some" of these components, take people on a journey from the WHY to the WHAT-IF, with WHAT as the ramp-up and HOW-TO as the meat.

- **35%** of people out there learn based on **Why**... the REASON this is relevant

- **22%** of people are **What** learners who understand based on ideas and facts

- **18%** of people learn based on the **How-To** of doing

- **25%** of people are **What-If's** who understand best through trial & error as well as the possibilities

If you limit yourself to just one of these learning styles in the sequence, for example, How-To... then you're only resonating with 18% of people out there. And even then, not very well!

In my line of work as a computer programmer, I constantly find myself in situations where I need to document a technical series of steps. Often, these instructions are for my future self to look at in 6 months, when I've completely forgotten what to click or type to use a special computer program.

When I was younger, I'd simply list the steps, the How-To portion. I'd record a video saying, here are the ten steps to setting up a website. I'd quickly show each click-through required to get the job done. The problem: I was STILL completely confused when watching my own instructions.

Maybe you've watched a YouTube tutorial with hesitation, thinking to yourself... is this the right video that solves my problem? Am I in the right place? What's this building up to? *(Side note: when you watch a recipe video on YouTube, isn't it more helpful when you see the finished product AND see the ingredient list before jumping in?)*

Many people (possibly you) have some idea of what the "meat" of their presentation (again, written, spoken, video, etc.) is, but you need the proper structure in place for it to really make sense.

One Problem, One Solution

One of the most helpful videos I ever watched was literally published by an 8-year-old (at the time). It showed how to record green screen video. It turns out that it came down to using the proper video software and clicking just the right button.

Let's say you were teaching the same thing. You want to show people how to record green screen (chromakey) video, but you don't want to pontificate about the history of green screen video or create a long, rambling intro. You also want these complex steps to make sense.

How do you structure something like this?

The Why Section: Here's why you'd want to record green screen video in the first place. It looks cleaner and more professional. Here are some samples of videos with and without green screen. This is WHY you want this.

The What Section: Explain the concepts and tools you're about to use so that the upcoming how-to section makes sense. Here's what we're about to do so you know you're watching the right video. Here's the software I'm going to use, here's the camera, here's the green sheet I'll hang behind myself. Here are some concepts you need to know about such as three-point lighting and shadows.

The How-To Section: First, show what the end result should look like. List the steps you're about to take, then switch gears and perform those steps. You may need to step back for a second and say... now we're on step 4, which is "this." Or, we're about to start step 6, so let me quickly list steps 1, 2, 3, 4, 5, which we've completed so far. After you've shown the process of you recording that video, applying green screen (chromakey), and processing the finished video, recap those steps you took so that it fully makes sense.

The What-If Section: Turn the "selling juice" back on and get people excited to use this newfound knowledge. Explain next steps, possibilities, maybe one advanced concept you left out. Show how green screen can be used with solid backgrounds, stock photography, animated video backgrounds, to display more information, and more.

Do you see how applying the WWHW structure can frame your instructions in the proper context, avoiding both the "jumping into the steps" trap AND avoiding the "padding" trap?

Listen to radio ads, TV commercials, or watch web pages that sell products. All successful ads follow the formula of Attention, Interest, Desire, Action: an attention getting headline, interest to align with their emotions and relate to their problem, desire to introduce your solution, and action to tell them to take action now. If you think about it, AIDA conforms to WWHW perfectly: Why is this important? What is the problem you're about to explain? How is this problem solved? And what-if I buy this solution right now?

I apply the WWHW formula in the book chapters I write, including this book! I apply WWHW in the online courses I sell, which show how to stream on Facebook, record podcasts, and publish books. Anytime I have any sort of presentation that's falling flat, I step back and ensure WWHW is in place, and in the proper order.

Abstraction

I once had a friend in college who claimed to be a "master speechwriter." (Spoiler alert: he wasn't.) After class, I asked to see his process in action. He played an audio clip on his laptop and began typing up every sentence that he heard. His "process" was simply to take each sentence and re-word it slightly. Terrible! Borderline plagiarism.

Twenty minutes later, he was still listening to minute one of a one-hour presentation.

If you're stuck about what to write or say, WWHW will get you out of that jam. It also works to beef-up any existing presentation you have. Many times, you already have the diamond in the rough content and you simply need to re-arrange, re-size, or re-work the pieces to make it hit hard.

Let's start with that first logical step of ensuring that your written materials, webinars, stage presentations, web pages, and tutorials start with a BANG... without losing your audience from the get-go.

Chapter 2: *Why* Is This Important?

Objective: Get attention, setup the problem that you're about to unpack further, and setup a "paradigm shift."

Are you the slightest bit afraid of being boring? Are you concerned that you have something interesting to say, but you'll start off on the wrong foot as soon as you start talking? What if your audience's attention continues to drop? Even worse, what if you completely "blank out" and stammer around for a few minutes until you find your groove?

Solution: Ask yourself this question... what's the goal?

Here's how to begin with impact: setup a real, powerful, urgent, emotional problem.

Don't begin with "hello." Don't begin with your name, your history, your credentials, the title of your presentation or even the problem you're solving.

The keyphrase to keep in mind for the *Why* section: "**Are you still _____?**" As in, are you still overweight? Are you still broke? Are you still unhappy? This mind-trick will help you to develop an interesting jumping-off point.

Problem, Agitate, Solve

Here are some headlines I've noticed from today's front page of the newspaper:

- Major Hurricane Could Threaten U.S. East Coast

- Homeless Veteran Could Get the $400,000 Owed to Him

- Do Men Exaggerate Their Number of Sexual Partners?

- How an Emergency Facebook Post Saved Travelers' Lives

Headlines on newspapers, magazine covers, and web pages are designed to get your attention. You're ultimately looking for your **HOOK:** something catchy, short and to the point that immediately draws people in to what you're presenting. That hook could be setup by your **Why** headline, and unpacked in your **What** section later.

If you don't grab your audience (in person, on YouTube, students, paying customers, your boss) immediately, then they're not going to pay attention to the rest. The point of your **Why** section (web page headline, speech opening line, YouTube video title) is ONLY to get them to keep reading! (Ever heard of "clickbait?")

The Greased Slide (Micro-Commitments)

In copywriting, we call this a "greased slide" or "bucket brigade." Just concern yourself in these first 30 seconds with getting their attention for 3 more minutes. Here are some other quick headlines:

- From Cosmo Magazine: "Killer Cocktail: How a Popular Drink Could Kill You in Your Sleep"

- One of the best attention-getting headlines of all time: "They Laughed When I Sat Down at the Piano, But When I Started To Play!"

- A hypothetical "Who Else" headline for weight loss: "Who Else Wants to Lose 10 1/2 Pounds in 4 Weeks, Have More Energy, Feel Better & Younger, and Do It All Without Dieting or Exercise AND In Just 3 Minutes Per Day?"

- Something more low-key for a YouTube video I could create: "I'm about to show you how to setup an Amazon cloud installation including a web server, database, and WordPress website."

The point is that you figure out what that "audience" wants (not needs), and give them something right away that you know they'll love.

In a live, in-person speaking environment, my usual go-to's are to: ask an interesting question to get them thinking, make an outlandish promise, or drop them in the middle of the action within a story.

Question: "What would you do if you only had 24 hours to live?"

Promise: "I'd like to show you how to get your website up and running, with all the bells-and-whistles, in just 5 minutes and in only 3 steps, using free tools."

Story: "Imagine my dismay when I reached for the toilet paper roll, only to discover there was just one small square left."

Opening Gambit

Consider how every *James Bond* movie starts with the opening gambit, right in the middle of the action. *In medias res!* The movie *Fight Club* began at the end of the movie, in a 30 second or so flashforward, and then rewound and began the movie. The movie *Star Wars: A New Hope* did a wonderful job of beginning in the middle of the action. What are these ships having a laser fight? Who are these guys in helmets dying left and right? Who's this guy in the black cape? Who's this princess, and these robots? What spaceship are they escaping? Start right with the action.

Don't skip the "Why" section. It's essential to get their attention. When speaking in-person, I'll be more showy and story-focused. But, when documenting technical tasks with screenshots, or demonstrating something in screencast format, I'll still emphasize the importance of paying attention: if you incorrectly configure your Amazon server (by skipping my instructions) then it will cause you huge problems down the road.

Wait until the tail-end of **Why** to introduce yourself, your credentials, and the title/thesis/goal of your presentation. Think of it like a TV show: the "teaser" act hits you with the action for a few minutes, and THEN they hit you with the opening credits, at which point the show has earned your attention, and can take its time building up with a slower first act.

To recap:

Start with a bang: something your audience relates to that can later relate to their wants, needs, and desires.

This story needs to be EMOTIONAL. The most straightforward approach is panic and fear. Talk about a time you were late, unprepared, or were lacking the necessary tools to get the job done. It could be hypothetical or a story about a friend. It could be something embarrassing that happened to you 10-20 years ago.

Intentional Chaos: Wake People Up With Weirdness

The MORE this section stands out like a sore thumb, the better. Wake people up with weirdness. Let's say you're presenting at a conference about the ketogenic diet where speakers have been talking about protein, fat, and lipids. You could ask, "What does Marty McFly from *Back to the Future* have to do with losing weight?"

Show vulnerability, use imagery, and, if you can, tell a story where you interact with others.

The most boring speech opener I've ever heard was from someone describing how he sat in a room, alone, trying to decide which college to attend. No! Tell me how the clock was ticking away, beads of sweat pouring down your forehead. Your Dad grabbed you by the collar of your shirt shouting for you to pick one. You imagined two parallel lives playing out, College 1 or College 2. You ran at full speed to the mailbox to mail that latter.

Once you've established this "wow" and you've wrapped up that quick story, introduce the problem you've setup, state you'll solve it, but don't solve it yet.

Now that you woke them up and pointed out the problem, introduce yourself. State your name, what you do, and why you're qualified to talk about this subject.

Introducing yourself at the end of your **Why**, when people are asking, "Who the heck is this person?" has that dramatic impact you're looking for.

Paradigm (Mindset) Shift

If you're still having trouble with this **Why** section (about 5 minutes for a 1 hour presentation and about 1-2 minutes for a 10-20 minute presentation), here's my usual go-to: tell a quick story about how you changed your mind about something. *A mindset shift!*

A fun one I use sometimes when teaching web pages is: I'll ask, "Which is more important about a website: the design or the text?" I show a slide containing a web page, but then show side by side: the text from that web page with no graphics, and the web page ONLY with graphics and no text. Now which one is better? The ugly website!

"Yield Sign" Opener

Ray Edwards is one of my favorite marketers. He uses the **"yield sign" opener.** I first read about this in a blog post by Dr. Steve McVey, so I don't feel bad about stealing it.

You ask your audience what color a stop sign is. Red. Then ask, what color is a yield sign? The usual answer, yellow.

(Pictured: A yellow yield sign. If you're not seeing this in color, just pretend it's yellow)

Then, show a picture of the "old" yellow yield sign that was used pre-1971. There's a problem... the yield sign we use post-1971 is red and white.

(Pictured: A red yield sign with a white interior.)

The point: not everything is as you remember. It's the "Mandela Effect." It may be time to re-consider limiting beliefs.

"The Last Starfighter" Opener

Another friend, Chuck Hooper of <u>SpeakerPresenter.com</u>, has what you could call **"The Last Starfighter" opener.** You win a high score at a video game and government agents knock on your door. They say, "That game was actually a simulator for a craft we need you to pilot to destroy an asteroid that's about to collide with the Earth and obliterate humanity."

Would you do it? Of course. But then the scenario changes to... what if it was a smaller asteroid that would only wipe out Africa's population of 1.25 billion people. You'd never meet any of the people you saved.

Would you still do it? It's a thought-provoking opener that transitions into a speech about how urgent it is that you donate to cancer research, to save the lives of people you don't know.

"Pop Quiz" Opener

Another respected mentor and marketer, Katrina Sawa of JumpstartYourMarketing.com, has one that involves taking a **pop quiz.** She passes out sheets of paper that has the numbers 1 through 50 scattered throughout. The test is to spend 60 seconds trying to circle each one in order. First, circle the number "1" which is placed randomly on the page. Then, find the "2" to circle and so on, until you get to 50. Most people can circle 30 to 40 of those numbers in the time allotted.

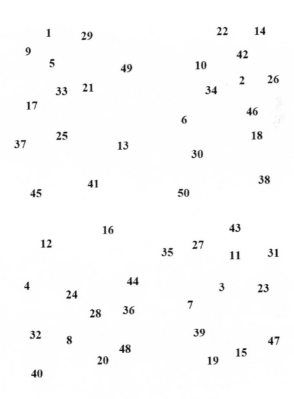

Katrina has you flip the paper over to see the same set of numbers 1-50. She explains the pattern: each number is in a different quadrant of the sheet of paper. The number "1" is in the top left corner, the "2" is in the top right corner, "3" is in the bottom right, and "4" is on the bottom left. And so on!

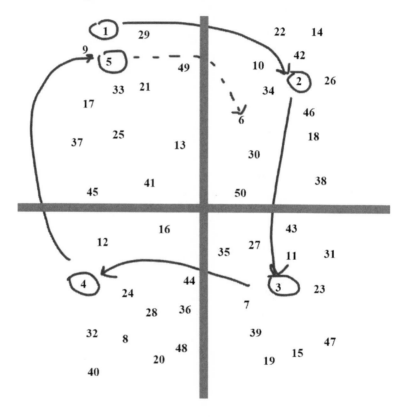

The audience is given 60 seconds to circle the numbers 1, 2, 3, 4, 5, all the way up to 50. The result: with the same problem, but one new piece of information, most people completes the challenge in 45 seconds. When a mentor provides you the guidance showing you the pattern (or where to focus), you get more done quickly.

Open Loops

When someone begins their presentation with a question, a motivational quote, or a joke, they're looking to get a PATTERN INTERRUPT to jolt people awake.

I'll admit this weakness: I constantly remind myself to add personal details, heart, vulnerability, and STORIES into my presentations. People love stories. (The way our ancestors communicated.) They're addicting, especially if you give lots of fun reasons to keep reading (or listening) and make it about things "they" can relate to. Bonus points if you "open loop" -- begin with the action and leave it unfinished, until later in your presentation.

Now that you've earned a few minutes of attention, how do you ensure the rest goes smoothly?

Chapter 3: *What* Do You Want Me to Know?

You're looking to present some information, be exciting, engaging, and entertaining... BUT how do you ensure that you're not too off-topic (goofy), AND that you get to the important parts quickly, AND that you're not moving so quickly that you're losing your audience's attention?

Objective: Create context for the problem you're about to solve, or the journey you're about to take. Make it obvious at the end (of the entire presentation, not just this section) when the problem (described in this section) is solved. Market the problem.

I realized that context was king when I had to take high school classes I didn't like. Running empirical formulas in chemistry class. Calculating cosines in math class. I wish I had been told **What** the usefulness of those things were before having to slog through hundreds of those problems for homework.

Keep this keyword in mind during the **What** section: **IMAGINE**. Imagine you had a money-making website. Imagine you smiled every time you checked your bank account. Imagine if doing your taxes was easy.

Deliver What They Want
(WIIFM, What's In It For Me?)

Dumb it down even if it makes you uncomfortable. I used to think that I had to appear as smart as possible: speaking quickly, throwing out fancy words, and cramming as much as possible into a short presentation.

In the computer programming world, we have a concept called "eating your own dog food." It's a visually disgusting way of saying that dog food tastes terrible because humans don't eat it. If you personally had to eat canned dog food, and yet you had control over its ingredients and preparation, you'd ensure it was edible.

Years ago, I was in a panic. A very well-known marketer had sent a flood of visitors to my humble little website without warning. Previously, I had setup a few pages on the site and hoped for the best.

With thousands of people clicking around at the same time, I realized that unless I had lead capture in place, I'd lose those thousands of visitors, never to see them again. I hurriedly tore down some navigation to make other things obvious.

In hindsight, it was strange that when only 20 people were visiting my website a day, I didn't care about delivering an optimized (SIMPLE) experience to deliver solutions to the problems that brought people to my website. When 5,000 people were buzzing around on the site, suddenly, I cared.

I had another "ah-ha" that same year when running a small in-person conference in Dallas, Texas. I spoke about content creation (blogging) and an attendee asked how to drip content. He wanted to know what tools or plugins to use in order to write 100 articles and schedule them out over a period of 100 days.

My answer to him: install WordPress (a blogging platform) on your website. Write your blog post. As you're about to publish that post (make it live), edit the date of your post and set it to one day in the future, and THEN publish. Because that post is future-dated, it won't appear UNTIL that specified date. Write another quick blog post. Set that post's date to two days into the future. And so on. No special plugins or tools required, completely built-in. He was so amazed (and I was amazed at HIS reaction) that I used that advice in future articles.

Sometimes people only need to know where to go and what to click. You may think advice like that is simple because you learned it ten years ago. But if people are frustrated because they can't find that simple answer, and they're desperate for a solution, give it to them!

Keep it Simple &
Don't Be Afraid to Re-Explain

A short time later, I attended a live online training webinar run by one of my students. She was teaching how to build an email list using a subscriber form on a website. I arrived at the 1-hour webinar 10 minutes in, and the screen was filled with gobbledygook and code. I'm a computer programmer, and even I was overwhelmed by what I saw!

She began using terms like "AWeber" and "email integration" and "follow-up sequences" which made things confusing in so many ways: I wasn't sure what we were building, I didn't know what I was looking at and I wasn't 100% sure I understood what was happening. This could have been remedied by taking a little time to explain what was being built, and what some of these terms like "AWeber" meant.

In other words, this person skipped the **What** section and jumped right into the **How-To** or the meat of that presentation. Fast-paced, but confusing as heck.

Picture this scenario: Robert Plank is giving a talk about email autoresponders. I ask, "Does everyone here know what an email autoresponder is?" Let's say half of the hands go up. Maybe I want to see if the lack of hands is simply due to shyness and non-participation. I could then ask, "Does anyone here NOT know what an email autoresponder is?"

Half of the people raise their hands, so this is an engaged room consisting of people with various skillsets. You might also have people who THINK they know what an "email autoresponder" is but have a different idea about it. Or, there could be attendees with a slight understanding of an "email autoresponder" but it's not at an expert level, so they didn't think they were worthy of claiming sufficient understanding.

The pickle I find myself in: do I re-explain email autoresponders or not? If I do, I'll bore the people who already know, and if I don't, I'll confuse the people who don't. Here's the solution: **reframing.**

I'd say, "It looks like most of us already know what an email autoresponder is, but just to make sure we're all on the same page, it's this." This way, it's explained in simple terms, it doesn't take up a lot of time, and no one is left out.

That "email marketing" presenter could have taken a few minutes to explain: here's what an email autoresponder is, the service I use is AWeber for this reason, here's what a signup form looks like, here's what an email blast is. Possibly, draw a diagram or have an easy to remember acronym. **Bonus:** re-visit this diagram or acronym multiple times later in your presentation so that it sticks.

Here's how I'd explain an "email autoresponder" to a crowd of doctors, whether they knew about them or not... I'd say:

- **Here's why you'd want to use an email autoresponder:** There are 5.6 billion email accounts, 99% of consumers check email daily, 50% check email 10 times daily, and the average person reads 140 emails per day. Email followup is the most underrated marketing tool at your disposal.

- *What you need to know about email autoresponders: how to build a list (collect patient email addresses), how to send a "blast", and what an email sequence is, where someone receives a special message on day 1, day 2, and day 3 after signing up.*

- **How it could be done, a real scenario:** Mary visits your office January 1st and agrees you can use her email address to keep in touch. On February 1st, a message is sent to see how she's doing. On March 1st, an automated message asks if she'd like to schedule another appointment. Patient John visits June 1st. Your system sends the "How Are You Doing?" message on July 1st, and asks if he'd like to return August 1st.

- **What if you setup an email autoresponder:** What if, out of the patients who visited your office but never returned, 30% of them now come back because you kept in touch, and didn't have to lift a finger?

Setup the Problem
(Fighting Against a Common Enemy)
That "We" Are Solving Together

Here's what you're looking to accomplish in the **What** section. (If you remember, the **Why** grabbed their attention and then introduced you as the expert.) In this phase, you're:

- Clearly stating the problem that needs to be solved and explaining the steps that led you to this point and/or the ALTERNATIVES you tried that failed.

- Breaking down the pieces or steps to the upcoming solution, but DON'T get into the steps just yet. Make people aware of what tools will be used to solve this problem.

- Explaining key tools, terms or concepts that you'll apply later. Make sure to NOT list out tons of terms. This isn't a glossary. It's just to get everyone on the same page about the words or phrases you'll use that may cause confusion later. It could be a good time to use an analogy or two to make it super-clear.

Circling back to the "email marketing" case study, the **Why** section could ask... what would you do if you lost your business tomorrow? And you had 30 days to rebuild everything in order to pay your bills. What would you do?

The answer is: I'd have it all back in 30 days because I have this skill to build a list. I'm Robert Plank, and I'm here today to show you how to build a list so that you don't have to work so hard on your business.

The **What** section could then unpack:

1. Why do I even need an email marketing list? Explain the pitfalls of not building that prospect or customer list.

2. Why do I need to pay for an autoresponder system? Show the hard way, perhaps the way things were done 10 years ago, that involves a lot of work and not a lot of results.

3. What about Facebook? Show the drawbacks of relying on social media or some other platform for your traffic.

4. You've convinced me that I need an email autoresponder... now what do I need to know? What (basic) terminology should I know and what pieces do I need to setup?

Use Alternatives (That Don't Work) to Move Your Presentation Forward

Another speaking friend, Rick Butts (rest in peace) used this template for his **What** section: Explain the problem that needs to be solved. *List the 3-4 most popular methods that did not work and why those failed.* All that's left is MY solution, which I'll then explain in the **How-To** section.

If you're following along, the **What** is: unpacking the problem, dishing out bad solutions, justifying the correct solution, and then setting the stage for a few of the words and steps that will be important in the **How-To** section. Here's how it fits into the Big Picture:

- **Why section:** gets attention, states the problem but does not yet unpack it

- *What section (current stage): unpacks/describes the problem at hand, introduces the solution but does not quite unpack it yet*

- **How-To section (coming up):** we're beyond "problem" mode and are unpacking the solution (the steps) to solve this problem, but we end with the problem of not knowing how to implement these steps!

- **What-If section (call to action):** give that push to take action and solve that problem

You're bridging the gap between the attention-getting fun of the **Why**, with the seriousness of **How-To**. It helps me to think of this in terms of "selling." The **Why** section sold people on why they should perk up and pay attention. In the **What**, I'm NOT selling the solution. I'm selling the problem and what does NOT work. They can probably relate to many of the frustrations that come along with building an audience or losing weight.

Let's try a quick exercise and apply the **What** section (importance, alternatives, justification, terms) into a weight loss presentation about the ketogenic diet:

> *Most of us want to lose weight for one reason or another: to look better, impress the opposite sex, maybe an upcoming high school reunion or wedding. Let's face it: losing weight is TOUGHER than it used to be! (relay some facts & figures to drive the point home)*
>
> *First, I simply tried not eating but that didn't work because my metabolism caught up with me, I was miserable, I didn't feel well, and it was unhealthy.*
>
> *Then, perhaps like you, I went on a diet. But that was expensive, required a lot of attention to detail, I didn't want to stick to it, I plateaued, and the effects were only temporary for these reasons...*
>
> *I tried exercise but that was time-consuming and that didn't stick for these reasons...*

I realized I had it all wrong. I met up with a friend I hadn't seen since high school. I remember he was always overweight, but he looked thin, healthy, and happy. I found out that he'd recently lost 27 pounds of fat, gained 8 pounds of muscle, and lost 5 inches from his waist. He was doing this, this, and this. The ketogenic diet.

Before I jump into how to apply the ketogenic diet, let me explain a few things just to make sure we're all on the same page. You might have heard some of these terms before, but let me tell you EXACTLY what I mean when I mention: ketosis, ketones, intermittent fasting, healthy fats, etc.

You might be thinking... do I need this section? Can't I jump into **How-To**? You're worried that you'll lose attention because you're too slow, and this is completely unfounded!

If you think you're losing attention, add jokes or randomness to get attention back every 10 minutes or so. You're repairing the bottlenecks where you lose people.

There is huge value in the fundamentals, and even your advanced audience members will benefit from getting re-introduced to some of those terms and basics they forgot about years ago, but were EXCITED about back then when it was new!

Market the Problem

Don't forget that the **What** section builds Interest, meaning that you're marketing the PROBLEM. Remember how the iPhone, the first all-touchscreen phone, was introduced? Steve Jobs didn't simply show the iPhone. He built up to it by showing pictures of Nokia and BlackBerry phones and their ugly, complicated keyboards, before showing the "real" solution.

As you get closer to the end of the **What** section (in a 1-hour presentation, about 15 minutes... in a 10-minute presentation, 3-5 minutes), remember this phrase: LET'S DO IT! (with the exclamation point)

If I'm presenting on a webinar about our *Make a Product* system, which shows you how to create and publish a book in a day, here's the structure I'd use:

Why (pattern interrupt) section: Tell a story like Roger Bannister's "Four Minute Mile" where no one thought any human could run a mile in four minutes, until it was done once in 1950, and then again and again. Another story is a lesson in simplicity and is about how the Space Shuttle ran on a 486 and floppy disks. I'm Robert Plank, I've published 12 books in the last few years, and I'd like to share with you today how you can publish a book, on any subject you want, 100% for free. Amazon simply takes a cut, and you can hold your own book in your hands in just a few days from now.

What (concepts) section: Explain how writing or ghostwriting won't work, the usual bad advice you get, and how self-publishing on Amazon is the best choice. But I need to explain what Kindle and CreateSpace are, what an ISBN number is, what they mean by "interior" and "cover." Then, let's do it! Let's go through the steps to get this book online.

Don't spend so long with your **What** section, that you're left with no time for the **How-To** or meat section. In a 1-hour webinar presentation, I'll spend 3-5 minutes on the **Why** to start things off, and 10-20 minutes on the **What**, so that I start the **How-To** demo halfway through the hour and have "plenty of time to take my time."

For an in-person 10-minute presentation, I'd spend no more than 2 minutes on the **Why** and 3 minutes on the **What**, leaving a good 4 minutes to explain steps and 1 minute with a close or call-to-action, the **What-If**. In a longer presentation extending to 20 or 30 minutes, I might spend 5-10 minutes on the **What**, but I still want to leave a LOT of room to explain the solution.

The "Stock Template" for Setting Up Your Concept

If you're still stuck about setting up the context around your solution, I have a simple format for you: **NO, OLD, NEW, RIGHT:**

- The people you speak to have a problem. What's life like with **NO** solution at all to that problem?

- Then, what **OLD** solution have they tried that's cumbersome, awkward, slow, expensive, and outdated?

- Then, what's a **NEW** solution that could solve the problem, but might not work due to being complex, incompatible, or too crowded?

- Finally, what is the **RIGHT** solution that you provide?

I'll give you an example: I recently had a guest on my podcast, John Jonas from OnlineJobs.ph. He explained the problem that happens when you hire people for your business:

- **"NO" Solution:** Your business has a lot of moving parts, and if you're working on it 24 hours a day, you'll be overworked, you'll run out of time, and you'll limit your own growth

- **"OLD" Solution:** The traditional thing to do is hire employees, buy office space for them, and now you have a ton of overhead and have no money left for yourself, PLUS you're spending time managing employees

- **"NEW" Solution:** Remote working is the hot thing these days, where you hire freelancers from around the world. The problem is that, although they are less expensive than employees, it takes time to train them, and after you've gotten to know the person, they've placed YOU on their backburner, have raised their rates, and may have moved on to new clients

- **"RIGHT" Solution:** Hire a Filipino worker who you will have to train but is extremely loyal and cost-effective for you

You could have a lot of fun and brainstorm all day about a concept you'd like to sell your audience on, simply by eliminating the alternatives that don't work. Think about it: by tackling things that don't work, you're relating to them in quite a big way.

You've been where they are, and possibly, you are showing that audience member a glimpse into their future, if they are on the "no" method, and will soon discover the "old" method, then stumble upon the "new" method, before finding the "right" solution.

The key here is not to make fun of the person, but to joke about the problem they have found themselves in. You're also looking to, if possible, stay away from IMPROVING something they're already doing, and instead say, you haven't gotten results not because your goal is bad or you're a bad person, but because the PATH you're taking to get to that goal is bad.

Another fun scenario that comes to mind: internet marketers landing local clients. We have friends Drew and David who have a concept called "Local Media Assets." Here's the setup:

- **"NO" Solution:** You're an internet marketer who has computer skills (setting up a website, getting social media traffic, etc.) but are always scrambling for money. You'd like some real business owners (restaurants, chiropractors, dentists, doctors, med spas) as clients so that you can apply those skills, and not only make a difference, but get paid what you're worth. The problem is that you don't have any of these local clients yet.

- **"OLD" Solution:** The old-fashioned way of landing a local client was to find a mom-and-pop business in town that needed a website. You'd create a simple website and get paid monthly for maintaining it. However, the marketplace is becoming extremely crowded as most businesses now have websites.

- **"NEW" Solution:** The next logical step is to grow and maintain (post content on) that business' Facebook, Twitter, and Instagram pages. Although most businesses need this, any internet marketer who has prospected has noticed a clear "have" and "have-not" divide: those businesses that don't have a social presence probably aren't interested in one, and those that do have a social presence are already taken by internet marketing agencies: your instant message is being received by their internet marketer, and not the business owner.

- **"RIGHT" Solution:** Drew & David's Local Media Asset concept involves building up your own traffic via social media, your own online newspaper, that you use to promote some local businesses around town, and get those looking for more foot traffic to come to you.

Any presentation is similar to the **three-act structure** used by movies, plays, and TV shows: beginning, middle, and end. The "beginning" was the **Why** and the first half of the **What**: selling the problem. The "middle" is where you transition into the solution (explain concepts in the **What**) and get to the real tutorial, coming up: the **How-To**. Examine the way I'm structuring the chapters in this book. Every chapter here is taking you on a journey: **Why** is this important, **What** are we going to do, **How** do we do it, and **What-If** we do it?

Chapter 4: *How* Do I Do This?

The moment you've been waiting for: listing out the steps or showing the steps in order to get a desired result. Your SOLUTION to the problem you're presenting about.

Objective: Explain the solution and the steps to getting from Point A (confusion, a problem not solved, or doing things the hard way) to Point B (a simple solution).

Let me remind you that WWHW only works on a per-chapter basis. Chapter 1 of your book, cycle through **Why, What, How-To, What-If.** Chapter 2, cycle through WWHW again. And so on. Do NOT ever have the "why" chapter, the "what" chapter, the "how" chapter, and the "what-if" chapter. That is the EXACT dull-ness you are trying to avoid.

(I realize the above scenario is EXACTLY how this book is laid out, but the ONLY reason for that is that WWHW is the concepts I'm explaining to you in our conversation today. In your own writing and presenting, you'd unpack each concept and cycle through WWHW within each chapter.)

An easy pitfall to avoid: I once overheard a marketer creating different webinar (PowerPoint) presentations. He created one just for the "why" people, one just for the "what" people, and so on. This also defeats the purpose. WWHW not only appeals to the different learning types, but it takes people on a journey from the **Why** (less specific) into the **What-If** (most specific, take this exact action). Ensure your presentations, essays, documentation, everything take the WWHW path from start to finish for maximum effectiveness.

The **How-To** section, or the demo. We're perhaps listing those ten steps to weight loss, or demonstrating how to upload a video to YouTube.

The key to a decent **How-To** section is this: tell them what you're about to show, show those steps, then re-cap the steps you just showed them. It may seem cumbersome for you to prepare and present, but trust me... this is going to make that presentation as powerful as it can be while still being accessible to newbies.

Consider the keyphrase, **"Let's Do It."** You've explained a three-step technique to combat schoolyard bullying. Instead of staying in theory-land, unpack an example so the concept makes sense in practice.

The Mechanics of Screencast Videos

To jump into the mechanics for just a second, I like to use Loom to record short videos and OBS (Open Broadcaster Studio) to create long-form information products. If you have a budget, Zoom.us is an excellent tool for recording your screen, web camera, both, or even another guest. And, if you'd like to show your phone's display on that computer screen, X-Mirage will do the job for Apple (iPhone & iPad) and Reflector for Android. You can see how we use these screen recording tools in our course at VideoSalesTactics.com.

The higher-end solution is one of my favorite pieces of software: **Camtasia Studio.** It records your screen but also has built-in editing capabilities. For screencasts, you'll also want to use either Microsoft PowerPoint (if you have it installed on your computer) or Google Slides (free and works in any browser).

Example: I first realized the importance of this while listening to a Tony Robbins self-improvement tape. He was explaining the six universal human needs: certainty, variety, love, significance, growth, and contribution. I remember thinking that it would have been so helpful if he had listed out those six talking points, unpacked each one, and then listed each one a final time. Far be it from me to tell Anthony-freaking-Robbins to change anything, but that's a little bit of repetition that my brain would have appreciated.

Here's what to do in your **How-To** or "demo" section:

1. Quickly explain what the demo is and what "we're" going to do (show a title slide in PowerPoint or Google Slides) -- When I present, I like to say that "we" are doing this, so pardon the awkward phrasing.

2. In bullet points, list out the starting point, what "we'll" click or type, and what the end result will be

3. Show those clicks taking place

4. Switch back to that PowerPoint presentation and re-state those steps that transpired

Our company sells a WordPress plugin called *Backup Creator*. In the free webinar that demonstrates the software and asks them to buy it, we show a PowerPoint slide that says:

1. We will login to our WordPress site and install the Backup Creator plugin

2. Enter our license key

3. Click "Backup"

4. Download the backup to our computer

5. Set offsite & automatic backup options

6. Switch off PowerPoint and login to website, then perform the steps. If it takes longer than 10 minutes,

switch back to the PowerPoint slides and show which current step "we" are on.

I hope it's easy to see how this translates to a written report and to a live stage presentation. **Example #1:** Here are five foods you should never eat when looking to lose weight and gain muscle. List all five foods. Unpack each of the foods for a few minutes apiece. Recap all at the end to make it stick.

Example #2: A screencast (Facebook Live stream, for example) showing how to upload a video to YouTube. The list of steps we're about to take: what to say in a video, how to record a quick video using your web camera, where to create a YouTube account, how to upload that video file, what to name that YouTube video, and how to share it on your Facebook page.

List the steps, show the steps, then list those steps again.

UseLoom.com is great for sending quick screencast videos. And, let's say you don't even have PowerPoint installed, or perhaps can't figure out Google Slides. Type your list of talking points in a Google Doc or Word document in large font. Place the list of text onscreen as you talk about them. It still gets the job done.

When documenting technical tasks on the computer... writing down the exact instructions or clicks to be made on the computer screen... I've found Google Docs combined with Jing Project (a screenshotting tool), a very useful combination. I can bring a computer screen exactly into the position I want, use Jing to draw a rectangle to capture some or all of that computer screen, add arrows pointing to areas of interest, click the button to Copy it to the clipboard, then switch back to the Google Doc, right-click and paste that graphic right onto the document.

In some other context, your **How-To** section (the meat) lists the steps you're walking them through. Examples:

- The Top 5 Drones to Buy This Christmas (the meat is the list of each drone)

- How to Lose Summer Fat in 5 Steps (the meat = the five steps)

- How to Record An Audiobook and Get Paid in 4 Steps (the meat = those steps to be performed)

If you look deep enough into your presentation, you'll see that it contains 3 to 5 steps in some way. Five steps, five types, one of four choices to make, or at the very least, three sections. The big takeaway is that a little repetition is okay to make things stick.

After you've setup your demo, demo'ed, and then recapped your demo, here's the keyword to wrap up the **How-To** stage: **INTRODUCING.**

Now that I've explained the steps to do this, here's the finished result. You must be wondering, what next?

Introducing... the solution to this problem. In a webinar pitch situation, the **How-To** section demonstrates long division and sells the calculator in the paid course, if you catch my meaning.

Introducing: the name of the solution that brings this solution together.

You've captured their attention, ramped up with terms and concepts, then demonstrated how to make progress. It's time to finish up...

Chapter 5: *What-If* I Put This Into Action?

How do you want to be remembered? (In your books, articles, emails, webinars, and presentations...) Keep this phrase in mind: **"call to action."**

Objective: End with a bang instead of a whimper, be remembered, don't overstay your welcome, and conclude with some sort of call-to-action.

You concluded the **How-To** section of your presentation with, **"Introducing..."** I've explained the steps involved in how to sell knick-knacks on eBay... introducing, my course. I have disarmed your fears about playing the guitar... introducing, my book that walks you through the process. You have just watched a module in my course showing the process of uploading a video to YouTube... introducing, your homework assignment or "challenge" to do it yourself.

Just as it was tempting to skip the setup of your presentation, it's also tempting to skip the end. **People need details!** If you're selling a course, take your time to explain why the course was created. State what result they'll get after completing the course. Explain what's in Module 1 or

Lesson 1, and how it relates to the entire solution. Unpack each module, explain bonuses if applicable, then recap the entire thing. The same applies if you're selling a book or simply convincing someone of an idea or action they should take. Explain the entire system, explain the pieces, then re-explain the entire thing.

My keyword-catchphrase to help with the **What-If** section is: **"Go Ahead, Do It Right Now."** Make the action you want me to take, 100% clear.

Your **What-If**, ending, call-to-action, doesn't always have to be a "monetary" sale. Salesman Grant Cardone would say that you are always selling in one form or another. Money does not have to change hands -- a "sale" could simply be persuasion. (Have you ever been "sold" on an idea?)

To expand on this concept: when you begin a presentation (of any kind, even a podcast) you are selling someone on the idea of listening for the first few seconds. Then, you are constantly selling that audience member *(Singular! Don't think about the masses -- think about the PERSON!)* to continue listening for just a few minutes more. You're selling people on your own credibility. You're micro-commitment-ing them to believe that the action you ultimately want them to take is a good idea, and that they can do it!

Example: You're selling a home study course about how to buy and flip raw land. The question in that audience member's mind isn't only, "Should I buy this course or not?" It's, "Will I implement this or will the course sit on my shelf? What if I back out? What if it's too hard? What if I don't make my money back? What if it's all a waste? What if I can't do it, not because the course sucks, but because I suck?"

If you aren't selling a course, if you aren't charging any money, and you simply want to make an impact on someone, or get them to take a simple action (floss their teeth, recycle their bottles, stop drinking diet soda) -- consider the **objections** that would hold them back from giving up before starting, and tackle them aggressively. Put as much effort into selling the idea as you would if you were asking for money.

This **call-to-action** could be a quick assignment for someone to take, a transition into the next chapter of your book, or simply a question for your audience to ponder now that you've explained this new information.

It's important to list features, but go into detail about the benefits. A "feature" is what it is: the name of chapter 7 of your book or module 3 of your course. The "benefit" is what someone gets from it. The result, the outcome, what they'll learn, what they'll do. Be positive. *Your **Why** section began with the bad, **What-If** will end with the good.*

End strong. Leave no room for confusion about the POINT you are trying to make.

Tell them what action to take now that you've delivered this information. Ask a thought-provoking question. Instruct that person listening/reading to "keep this in mind the next time you're in this situation." Or, the next time THIS happens, do THAT instead.

- You've given a presentation about the three types of schoolyard bullying. Explain that the next time they observe bullying or are bullied, **they can do "THIS."** Don't end by saying "thank you" or "bye." Do NOT end with a PowerPoint slide that says, "Questions?" or ask, "Any questions?" Reason: everyone does this and it doesn't stand out.

- You've written an article (and posted it to your LinkedIn account) regarding what business owners can do to be more organized with their accounting. **Call to action: implement this checklist, buy my book.**

- Webinar video presentation: how to create a money-making membership site. **Call to action: buy this online course that shows you how.**

Plan those 1-2 "ending" sentences ahead of time so that you finish strong. I was once interviewed on a podcast, and the host ended with this statement: "Thanks for listening, and I hope I didn't screw up this interview too much." Yuck! Successful YouTube stars (the ones with millions of subscribers) end their videos by telling you to comment, like, and subscribe. It works!

End with a call-to-action. Tell me to go to the back of the room to claim access or what website URL to visit next.

You might end a casual presentation by saying "do this in the future" or end a webinar by saying "go to this website."

A call-to-action could also take a few forms depending on what you're trying to accomplish. For example:

- At the end of an article, deliver a **list of tasks to perform** based on the new information

- When you end a book chapter, explain how to implement and **acknowledge the NEW problems it creates** -- the perfect transition into the next chapter

- Create a **quick (3-5 question) "pop quiz"** that asks questions based on what was just explained, so your readers can easily test their knowledge

This is the structure that makes the most sense for your writing and presentations: **Why** should I pay attention to what you're about to explain? **What** principles & concepts are you about to illustrate? **How** do I get this done, what are the steps? And **what-if** I do this, what is the next step?

If you're stuck on an ending for your presentation, article, podcast, webinar, or video, here are a few options:

Option #1: Full Circle. End where you began, circling back to your original point, having taken your audience on some sort of journey. Bonus points if you have a specific sentence or phrase to begin your presentation, and you re-visit that magic "phrase" multiple times throughout your presentation. (Icing on the cake: if that catchphrase rhymes, it's more memorable.)

Option #2: Point A to Point B. Instead of coming full circle, you take people on a journey where the end-point is drastically different from where you began. You could throw in a quick summary repeating everything that's happened: the problem, the setup, the steps to fix the problem, and where you ended up.

Option #3: Repeated Call-to-Action. You could call this "the hard sell" and is where you repeat, several times, the web address to visit or the "thing" you'd like people to do.

Option #4: Challenge or Assignment. Provide a specific task or action to be completed. When I teach a webinar class, I end a session by asking people to answer four quick questions that get them an inch closer to applying what they learned.

In a casual speech-delivering environment, you could close with a VERY short micro-story, joke, or motivational quote.

Chapter 6: *Present* to a Crowd Using the WWHW Formula

If you can't bring yourself to take a specific action, write it down. Perhaps you need to get clarity on it!

However, writing (and reading) will only get you so far. I realized at a young adult age that I could write all the blog posts in the world, but many people wouldn't read them, and if they did, they would only skim. I needed to be a live person. I needed to present in-person, in videos, webinars, and podcasts.

The keyword that helps me the most when speaking is: **UNPACK.**

Some people are concerned that if they present a 3- to 5-minute speech, it will be too short to "fit everything in." Likewise, you might be thinking about recording a 10-minute YouTube video to demonstrate a skill, but are concerned about giving too much away. The concept of unpacking ensures that you have the structure, the skeleton, the essentials, but you can choose to give the quick overview OR dive deep if you have a longer time-slot.

Years ago, I interviewed for an IT job at a university. (I landed the job.) In order to differentiate myself from other computer programmers applying for the same position, I told a story about a "split testing" software plugin I had created. I explained it like this:

Why **Section, Introduce the Problem:** In advertising, there's an old saying: "I know I'm wasting half my money on advertising, I just don't know *which* half." Recent studies have shown that it only takes people 50 milliseconds to form an opinion about a web page. It's also been proven (through EEG measurements of the brain) that after the invention of mobile phones, the average human attention span has dropped from 12 seconds to 8 seconds. (The attention span of a goldfish is 9 seconds.) Therefore, it's ultra-important to ensure everything on a web page is optimized.

What **Section, Explain the Concept:** The answer to this website optimization problem is not guessing, it's split testing! Split testing, or A/B testing in its simplest form, means that we show half of website visitors page "A" and half the website visitors page "B."

A copywriting friend, Ryan Healy, from RyanHealy.com, sent 50% of his website visitors to a web page that began with the words, "Dear Friend," and 50% to a web page without the words, "Dear Friend." Surprisingly, the version WITHOUT the words "Dear Friend" made 28.2% more sales. Because of the results of this test, he knew to permanently remove the words "Dear Friend" from his web page to enjoy a 28.2% increase in income. If that website had made him $1,000 per day, it was now making him $1,282 per day, just from removing two words.

How **Section, Tell a Story:** Here's how you would split test your webpage to increase what are called "conversions." You'd install my software and decide which variable to test. For example, send 50% of your website visitors to a page with a red headline, and 50% of your website visitors to a page with a blue headline. After thousands of people have visited both versions of the web page, you'll have a clear winner -- what the nerds call "statistically significant."

Let's say the red headline produces 2% more email signups, or even sales of a book, than the blue headline. You've now given yourself a 2% raise in income.

What-If **Section, Explain Possibilities:** When you split test your webpage, you are no longer guessing. Also, if page "A" converts even 1% or 2% better than page "B" -- then the winner of that split test becomes your "control." You throw out the losing page and keep the winning page. And then... rinse and repeat the process! Choose another "variable" to split test -- for example, send half your website visitors to a page with a white background and the other half to a light gray background. The worst case scenario: you'll continue to convert at your current levels.

In the above split testing example, I could rattle off that micro-story in 3 minutes in a job interview situation. If I had to give that presentation in a 20-minute podcast, I could spend more time in the **Why** section explaining the problem that split testing solves. I could use the **What** section to explain alternative split testing solutions. I could beef up that **How-To** section by adding additional stories, examples, and terms. I could lengthen **What-If** by asking additional questions or giving a quick assignment to ensure the listener takes action.

You can easily see how, by shortening or lengthening these sections (but keeping the WWHW structure) I can present the same information in 3 minutes, 20 minutes, or 90 minutes! I could even make the WWHW journey of "split testing" a single module in an all-day presentation in which I deliver four modules in a one-day workshop.

Writing is preparation, but it doesn't give you feedback. You can't adjust for a crowd, take your time along the way if they seem extra interested, or move on if they're bored.

Case in point: I was selling a $2,497 product in Thailand a number of years ago. My business partner and I had thoroughly rehearsed, were wearing matching $3,000 suits, passed jokes to one another, walked around the room, drew on flip charts using markers, delivered many wow's and ah-ha's. The audience was just not very engaged. We sold enough copies to make the trip more than worthwhile, but we didn't exactly light the room on fire.

The person presenting after us was a world-renowned motivational speaker who orated to crowds in packed stadiums regularly. Even *he* could not get the attendees very aroused. I thought to myself, "At least I know I'm not the problem!"

The third speaker wore an old faded t-shirt, baggy jeans (with a chain wallet), and flip flops. He had not yet showered that day, sat in a chair on stage (behind a laptop) and did not move from there. He began his presentation by apologizing for being hungover, and ended his presentation 14 minutes into a 60 minute speaking time slot.

He just about sold out the entire room! And went home with more money earned than the rest of us speakers COMBINED!

What was the difference?

He delivered what the audience wanted, which was point and click software that created an entire website funnel. The buyers in the room walked away in love with the idea that they could create boxes connected by arrows, in just a few clicks.

Chapter 6: Present to a Crowd Using the WWHW Formula

When you speak, choose your goal in advance. The four avenues of presenting are: to **Entertain**, to **Inform**, to **Persuade**, or to **Inspire**. Out of those four, choose just one primary focus and one secondary focus to "flavor" your speech. It doesn't have to be an info-dump.

A year after Thailand, I was about to present on stage in Las Vegas to a room of 150 people, competing against 8 others, for a chance to win $25,000. The speaking contest was called "Better Your Best." The premise: explain what you did to have the best year ever (income-wise) in your business, surpassing all previous years, and convince the room to vote for you as the winner.

One of the attendees had a very engaging PowerPoint presentation. Another used various props. Yet another had scripted the entire thing out and refined it 20-plus times over the previous month.

I won that competition, even though I had not prepared or practiced anything, and made it up on-the-spot. I have Hangover Guy from Thailand to thank for that! If not for him, I might have presented four tips, four steps, or four reasons to vote for me. Boring!

Instead, I used the WWHW structure for this four-minute presentation:

- **Minute 1 (Why):** I asked the audience if they had regrets or had lost someone close to them. I told a quick micro-story about my last week ever at a 9-to-5 job. My father, who lived out of state, was only 59 years old, secretly had cancer at the time, and died three months later, surprised me at work. I was glad to see him and told him I had "put in my notice" to quit that job. He had doubts, but I told him I had generated $32,500 in online income that month and would be okay. He was proud of me.

- **Minute 2 (What): I setup the problem.** Months later, I was fully self-employed but also experienced rollercoaster income, stress, and uncertainty. I needed a mentor.

- **Minute 3 (How-To): The solution.** I found a mentor, Armand Morin, who showed me how to implement "pitch webinars" to fill up my membership sites with buyers.

- **Minute 4 (What-If): The call to action.** I gave one last reason to vote for me and explained what I'd do if I won. I limited this section to 30 seconds so as not to go over time.

Here is the WWHW presentation structure in a more abstracted, templatized format so you can easily apply it yourself...

Minute 1, Why. Ask a question to wake people up. Get them thinking. Get a little personal and emotional. Say something attention getting, out of the ordinary, mindset shifting.

Be a little vague in this stage so that people fill in the blanks themselves. "Are you mad? Because I sure am." (Then continue to unpack that in this section.) "Have you ever struggled?" (Then dive deep into the emotion of that.)

This is important: **find something to agree about, so the rest of your presentation does not fall on deaf ears.** If you immediately insult your audience or contradict their pre-existing beliefs, they'll be turned off right away.

I was once presenting to a small room in Buffalo, New York, about membership sites. I asked, "Did you hate school? Raise your hand if you did." And I raised my hand. Hardly any hands were raised. Usually, when this happens, I then ask the opposite question, and if no hands raise, I ask, "Then who here won't raise their hand no matter what I say?" As a joke.

I asked, "Who here loved school?" Surprisingly, almost all the hands in the room went up. Without thinking, I blurted, "You guys are a bunch of nerds!" The point I was trying to make was that the membership site these people were about to create didn't have to be as "dry" as a classroom lesson in school could be. However, if I had a do-over, I would have said, "I liked school too. I really enjoyed [this] and [that] subject in school. However, I didn't like [this particular class] because it was too boring." There is a way to make your point without destroying common ground.

Dating gurus (Pick Up Artists) would say that it's easy to accidentally make a **Demonstration of Lower Value (DLV)** by being too nice, too arrogant, too eager, too fast, too slow.

You're looking to make a **Demonstration of Higher Value (DHV)** which does not always mean being the most helpful or "nicest" speaker your audience has ever seen. However, your conscience also won't allow you to deliver a complete "waste of time" presentation. The answer is to deliver what your audience wants and needs. **Entertain**, **Inform**, **Persuade**, or **Inspire** -- choose two.

Minute 2, What. Further explain the problem. Describe the various alternatives they've tried and perhaps those they didn't try. Make the hurt even worse. Get them practically begging for you to provide a solution.

Ask them questions and make it about them. This also eases your own nerves because the focus is not on you, but on this audience you are helping.

Minute 3, How-To. Explain an easy solution or step they can take to correct that problem or at least make progress.

Minute 4, What-If. What big lesson do you want people to take away from your talk? If you don't have an answer, let me give you an easy one: "Keep _____ in mind the next time you _____."

Your **What-If** asks people to think about things differently or take some sort of action. End on a high note. Put some thought into your first and last sentences.

Three to five minutes is a great length of time to make a quick point. If you're speaking within a longer time slot, keep the ends (**Why** and **What-If**) the same length, but add sub-points to your **What** and **How-To** segments.

Consider adding transitions or callbacks (references to earlier parts of your speech) to really make your point. Add jokes if they present themselves.

Robert Cialdini's Six Weapons of Influence

If you're looking to make your presentation the best it can be (no matter what length) allow me to give you six pieces of advice: Robert Cialdini's Weapons of Influence. (You can find out more about this in his very excellent book "Influence.") When I'm looking to really punch up my presentation, I check to apply these six principles:

Principle #1: Reciprocity. When you do someone a favor, they are obligated to give you something in return. Can you offer something for free? Or deliver some very valuable information with a clear benefit?

Principle #2: Commitment and Consistency. Can you get someone to agree with you on something small before asking for a larger commitment? Can you get an easy "yes" or two? Ensure you're keeping their attention. Perhaps ask if it's okay to share this or help solve that.

Principle #3: Social Proof. People are more interesting than facts or things. Do you have any interesting stories involving other people to make your point? No one wants to hear you brag. Explaining how someone else benefitted, did something, or taught something, makes it more pleasant to hear.

Principle #4: Liking. Have you ever dealt with a person who seemed really smart, but you had no idea why? Perhaps they dressed like you, spoke like you, and had similar beliefs as you. On the other hand, if someone spoke faster (or slower) than you, had some wacky ideas, and didn't establish rapport, you wouldn't be as receptive to what that person had to say. People like others who are like them, and this is where "finding common ground" (as previously mentioned) works wonders.

Principle #5: Authority. I delivered a presentation and an audience member told me she didn't believe me because I mentioned statistics without sources. This person was well educated and had a habit of mentioning her various credentials. Nothing wrong with that. Different people think in different ways.

Principle #6: Scarcity. Many people can be interested and even convinced, but won't take any action unless there's a deadline, an offer about to disappear, limited quantity or a price about to rise. You can also use scarcity in your positioning in that only a few people know about the information you're about to deliver, as a sort of shared secret, or exclusive club that very few people know about.

Look at your presentation and ask yourself if you apply adequate amounts of reciprocity, consistency, social proof, liking, authority, and scarcity. Do you rely too much on one aspect? Do you lack authority in your presentation? Are you leaning too heavily on authority, and you need to counter-balance a perceived "snobiness" with liking or social proof?

Remember to have fun. Don't let jitters get to you. Person A can feel burnt out doing what they love (because their goals suck) and yet Person B can be completely fulfilled with the "drudgery" because the goal itself is fulfilling. In the same way, you can conquer the greatest fear of all time (public speaking) by keeping in mind the end goal: to get your message out there and help people.

If you're interested in presenting to a crowd (online), in the form of an online class, instructional video, or sales webinar, then you'll want to visit our WebinarCrusher.com online course to learn webinars and VideoSalesTactics.com to get the system we use for video recording and Facebook live streaming.

Speaking of using the WWHW formula to take the unpleasant action needed to get to a more pleasant goal, let's apply it to your greatest challenge yet: writing a book.

Chapter 7: *Write* an Entire Book Using WWHW

The paradigm (mindset) shift is what life is all about. What one single moment defines you? I'm guessing that no standalone event does! That would make you a one-note cardboard person, which sounds quite boring. You had many milestones and ah-ha's in your life to get to where you are. It was never about slowly progressing inch-by-inch to a goal, or winning the lottery and instantly getting there. It was about the various jumps along the way.

I want you to "write" your own book. When you have a book, you are instantly thought of as an expert, you have something people will hesitate to throw away, and you have an opportunity to show what makes you unique. Ah-ha's!

Writing became infinitely easier for me as soon as I abandoned the idea of "chapters." Sure, call the sections of your book "chapters" -- but not WHILE you're writing your book. Instead, the keyword to install in your mind is: **CONCEPTS.** Writing a book containing seven chapters sounds difficult. But what if you thought of a few concepts, explained each in **Why, What, How-To, What-If** format, and then renamed those "concepts" into "chapters" after you were done?

The books and other programs I've enjoyed the most were those that began with a simple concept in one chapter, and then built on other concepts as the next chapters progressed.

We've previously discussed how you can get over the boredom, anxiety and uncertainty of a task by leaning (slightly) on the structure to add some excitement back in. It's about discipline, not motivation! Have the discipline to get started and the motivation kicks in when you see progress. Even outlining or decision-making is progress.

The structure I use for a book is this: seven chapters total, with each chapter broken down into **Why, What, How-To, What-If** sections. In a blog post or live speech, we expanded WWHW to fit that length of time. But now, in long-form book content, we are iterating through WWHW in a series of seven ah-ha's.

It's okay to have a short book. In fact, I wrote this entire book on my iPhone (Google Docs) while out walking. Books these days are thin and to-the-point. Information moves much faster nowadays, self-publishing has made the marketplace much more competitive, and people are time-starved more than ever before. No one has time to read a long book. Plus, you don't have ten years to create that long book!

I believe that these simple techniques will make rapid book writing extremely easy for you:

- **Question-based thinking, as previously discussed:** outline your book as a series of questions and sub-questions to ensure a clear focus

- **Mindmapping:** pile in a flood of ideas (I call them the raw materials) that you can then rearrange, trim, and sub-categorize (S.C.A.M.P.E.R. thinking)

- **Countdown timer:** force your brain into time-limited fight-or-flight mode to force action-taking and decision-making

- **Transcription:** speak out your book in 8-minute increments (which will make sense in a moment) into audio format, then pay someone to transform that spoken audio into words (for $1 per minute) and cleanup the text afterwards. This allows you to see your book coming together with faster progress than ever before.

An "outdated book" is 30,000 to 50,000 words in length: 100 to 200 pages. The formula for a quick book that you can add to later, but gives you something that's complete for now, is: 35 pages, 7 chapters, 1 hour of speaking.

That's right: you can create a book (if you use a formula to minimize decision-making) from one hour of speaking. In fact, I once created a book in 12 hours, from idea to publication. I thought of the idea at 6AM, outlined at 7AM, narrated at 9AM, got the transcript back at 11AM, submitted it all by 2PM, and Amazon had approved it (available for purchase) by 6PM that same day. It is possible! That book is called "The Checklist Mindset."

What if you had one focused weekend, or even one week, where you created and published a simple book? You could always add another chapter here and there or even repeat this process to double the size of your book. Think outside the box!

Here's the exact process for a 3.5 hour book:

Hour 1: Outline

Decide on your book's hook: the overall problem you're going to solve in a unique and interesting way. What question lead people to your book? It should be answered after people read it.

What ten questions would people ask along the journey to solving this problem? Think of exactly ten. Don't go under or over. There's a value in stretching yourself and spending time plowing through questions one through three (the obvious ones), questions four through seven (the ones that suck), and finally, questions eight through ten (the really good ideas that you wouldn't have discovered if you hadn't plowed through those bad questions.)

Next, reduce those ten questions down to seven. The reason being that some of those questions you mindmapped really suck -- let's be honest! Delete the weakest questions you previously listed. If a question you asked is so good that you can't bear to delete it, could you combine it with another existing question? S.C.A.M.P.E.R. thinking from earlier comes in handy. If this isn't making sense yet, it will once you see it in action.

Break down each of these seven chapters (questions) into WWHW sub-questions. Let's say you were outlining a real estate book and one chapter was about buying and renting.

Question: What do I need to know about buying and renting a home?

Sub-questions: **Why** would I want to buy and rent compared to other alternatives? **What** concepts do I need to know about buying and renting? **How** do I buy and rent, what are the steps? After I buy and rent a home, **what** new opportunities does it open up?

Rearrange your chapters (questions) into an order that makes sense. I find that my books are usually structured with four "fundamental" chapters plus three advanced or practical chapters. If you come across a book of mine with more than seven chapters, I've probably added to it over time.

Optional: list three keywords (one or two words at most) to place alongside each of your seven chapter's WWHW sub-questions. This might be the most time-consuming part of building your outline, but it ensures you'll never get stuck, and that you'll be excited to speak out your book.

The final product of your outline will be: your title phrased as a question, worded as if a person is asking it to you. It's then broken down into seven sub-questions, with each sub-question broken down into **Why, What, How-To, What-If**, sub-sub-questions, optionally with three keywords listed to help you with the answers.

Hour 2: Recording

It's time to speak out your book. If you haven't narrated a book before, you might consider this the toughest and most important part, but if you have, you'd say this step was the easiest and LEAST important section.

Any recording process will work for this. I personally use Audacity Recorder, which is a desktop program that runs on Mac or PC. If you're more of an app person, install the Evernote app to record voice memos. If you prefer websites, Zencastr.com allows for free recording using any computer.

Hardware: use your computer's built-in microphone to get started now, a Logitech ClearChat headset ($25) if you're on a low budget, or a Blue Yeti microphone if you have a slightly higher ($120) budget. Don't overthink this. Just get recording. This is NOT an audiobook. No one will hear this raw audio recording except you and your transcriptionist.

The process: click the Record button, and read the question-title of that chapter aloud so it's fresh on your mind. Read the question within that chapter aloud and take two minutes answering it. You could speak for two minutes answering a question, couldn't you? Two minutes would be an extremely short phone conversation.

After you answer that question, feel free to stop and come back, or move onto the next question and record the entire chapter. The end result: a chapter recorded in eight minutes of audio (answering four questions: **Why, What, How-To, What-If**), times seven chapters for a total recording time of **56 minutes**. This equates to about 9,000 words, or 30 pages of a 6x9-inch printed book. Add a title page, table of contents, introduction page, your contact information, about the author bio, and a few pictures, and you're easily in the 40-50 page range. However, none of that matters, since Amazon KDP Paperback only requires 24 pages.

After you speak out and record your book, send it off to Rev.com for transcription. Rev only costs one dollar per minute, so a 56-minute recording only costs you $56. Many times, I'll go a little "over time" in my books and end up with a 70 or 90 minute recording. That's a perfectly good problem to have!

After your written transcript comes back, it's time to clean up that text and jump through just a few hoops (don't worry, not many) in order to get it online and selling on Amazon.

Hour 3: Editing

No transcript that comes back is perfect, so please, manage your expectations. For the price and speed, Rev comes back with some of the best transcripts I've seen, but you'll still need to make a few passes to remove all errors. The key is to make short passes to clean up your transcript:

- Search (control-F or command-F) for the word "inaudible" to fix any spots in the transcript your transcriptionist was not able to understand

- Remove repeat filler words including: and, because, just, like

- Remove or re-word instances of weak language like "sort of" or "kind of"

Make a quick pass to fix superficial errors: I like to set a timer and only allow myself one minute per page to fix things. It's all about multiple passes, not getting stuck making one section perfect.

Google Drive (Google Docs) is an extremely helpful tool for editing, because you can share with others (everyone can edit) or you can edit some on the computer, and edit more on your phone. The updates are instant.

Editing can be a lot of fun, almost like a game! You could scan a single page, identify the weakest sentence in each paragraph, and clean up just that paragraph. You could punch up the first and last sentence of each chapter. You could read your paragraphs backwards to ensure you have decent transitions.

You could print out your book and rate each paragraph on a score of 1 to 10, with 1 being the worst and 10 being the best quality. Get to work on just the 5 and 6 scored paragraphs.

If a paragraph is rated 5 or 6: read each sentence aloud to easily find the awkwardness and mistakes. Rated 7 or 8: locate 2-3 words that can be removed from each sentence to deliver the same message.

What's reassuring about self publishing is that you can always edit. Get your manuscript as cleaned up as you can make it in an hour, just enough to get it published, or at least to order "proof" copies your friends can review. Then re-upload the newer version. (Even a college textbook in its 10th edition has a list of "errata" found in the previous edition.)

Once your book manuscript is at "good enough" status, format your chapter titles by setting them as "Heading 1." (In either Google Docs or Microsoft Word.) Add a table of contents and title page. Optionally, add pictures, your contact information, and an About the Author chapter.

The place we're about to submit the book is KDP.Amazon.com. When you go to submit the book, they provide a ready-made Word document template.

Final 30 Minute Home Stretch: Publishing

The best news of all: publishing a book (both digitally and physically) is FREE! It's true. Amazon only takes a percentage of your book's selling price and sends you a check every month. There are no setup costs and no minimum order. People can buy your book on automatic pilot or you can purchase a big box of your books to hand out.

After you've created an account on <u>KDP.Amazon.com</u>, and clicked the button to add your "title" -- Amazon only needs a few pieces of information to publish your Kindle (digital) book:

Book Information

They'll want to know your book's title, your name as the author, as well as any additional names, i.e. the person who wrote your book's foreword. Add a description, which appears on the Amazon listing for your book -- just a few sentences about the problem the book solves.

Write a **Why** sentence (the problem that led someone to this book), a **What** sentence (what the book does overall to solve the problem), a **How-To** list (five to ten bullet points explaining specific exciting things they'll find in the book) and a **What-If** call-to-action (a command to buy the book now).

Amazon will ask (fairly early) about your ISBN number. Choose the simple option and have them provide a free one for you.

I guarantee that publishing a book will seem awkward the first time around, but it's almost impossible to make a mistake. Just step through the step-by-step process. You don't even need to be completely ready when you begin the book publishing process, as you can leave your half-submitted book in draft mode.

Cover

Your book needs a cover. The good news is that a Kindle (digital) book requires only a flat cover -- no spine or back cover. Even more good news: when it comes time to create your Kindle Paperback (physical), you can choose their special template that allows you to drop that flat cover in as the front cover, type in your bio for the back cover, and they will generate the spine (side of the book) for you.

These are the precise requirements for creating a cover graphic for Amazon:

- size: 2560x1600 pixels

- format: TIFF

- add text for title, subtitle, and your author name

- no text within 10% of the edges

If you're a graphics whiz and can create a book cover based on the above, congratulations! If not, visit Fiverr.com, search "kindle cover" and hire someone who looks like they do a decent job. Give them those above requirements. Look at a few book covers in your industry that you like the best. Give your worker suggestions based on colors, graphics, and any other ideas you have. Attach three book covers whose styles you prefer. That gives you a book cover!

Interior

In order to create a book, you must upload its inside pages. This means you need to add page numbers, a table of contents, title page, disclaimer page, possibly a Conclusion Page and About the Author Page.

When publishing your Kindle Digital version, save your manuscript as a Word document. Amazon will strip out the page numbers, because Kindle books can be resized. The font size can change, it can be displayed on a large tablet or small phone, so page number is irrelevant with that setup. When publishing your Kindle Paperback (which you should only do after your Digital version is submitted), save your manuscript in PDF format, and enable PDF/A compliance. You don't need to know what that means, but saving it in that way will avoid a few headaches down the road.

Amazon has you preview the book. They may give you a few warnings if your margins are too narrow, if they detect too many typos, or if the graphics are too low in quality. That last issue is not too major and can usually be ignored.

Marketplace

After your book details, cover, and interior are submitted (you may have to wait a few minutes for things to generate), continue stepping through the final tabs in this process. Amazon will ask what you'd like to price your book at (I usually choose $1.99 for Digital and $9.99 for Paperback), choose categories and keywords for the book (don't overthink this), and which countries it will be sold in -- all of them! Submit and wait for Amazon's approval, which sometimes takes 48 hours, but they've approved me in as little as 2 hours.

Case Study: "Mind Hacking"

Do you want to go along the journey with me as I map out a real book? I thought so! Let's outline a book called mind hacking. I'll walk you through my process, including research.

I want to create a book that deals with issues of the mind: aging well, getting focused, having energy, sleep, improving memory, mood, and weight loss. I'll perform a few Google searches to find "listicle" articles, and scour Amazon for a few similar books to peek at a few table of contents sections to see some similarities and overlaps.

It's key not to copy anything and not glean from one single book. You're quickly flipping through the table of contents of several books to see what topics appear again and again. Search Amazon for "mind hacks"... click into a few different books, click the book cover, then use the popup that appears to see that book's table of contents.

Looking for ten questions, here's what I created for you...

Title: How can I have the best mind possible?

1. How can I be happy, think more positively and overcome self-sabotage?

2. How do I focus better, live in the moment, and listen to what people say?

3. What is lucid dreaming and how can I use it to better solve problems?

4. How do I learn faster and improve my memory, especially as I get older?

5. How do I adopt good habits, act quicker and make better decisions?

6. How can I get excited about the work I'm doing and avoid boredom?

7. How do I avoid procrastination and perfectionism?

8. How can I reduce my anxiety?

9. How can I be better disciplined?

10. How do I increase my confidence and become more self-sufficient?

I've listed ten questions, all worded as if someone is asking them of me, listed in the order I thought of them. I particularly like the "anxiety" and "confidence" questions. You might also notice that questions are problems to be solved. They aren't boring (vague) topics like "mindfulness" or "reading" or "sleep."

The next step is to reduce this list down to seven questions. I thought of, and listed, ten questions, and it's time to squish things down to seven. This means that I can completely delete a question if it's weak or repetitive, or combine a question into another if it's too painful to remove. It also means that if a question in the above list is too good to remove from the outline, I can choose a weaker question to take off this list.

1. How can I find my life purpose, get excited, be happy, avoid boredom, think more positively and overcome self-sabotage?

2. How do I focus better, live in the moment, and listen to what people say?

3. What is lucid dreaming and how can I use it to better solve problems?

4. How do I learn faster and improve my memory, especially as I get older?

5. How do I adopt good habits, act quicker and make better decisions?

6. How do I use discipline to avoid procrastination and perfectionism?

7. How do I reduce my anxiety, increase my confidence and become more self-sufficient?

I rolled the "discipline" question into the "procrastination" one, rolled "anxiety" into confidence and rolled "excitement" into "happiness."

Re-order these into something that makes sense. This part is a matter of what looks correct. I tend to group the book into four easy chapters and three advanced ones:

1. How can I find my life purpose, get excited, be happy, avoid boredom, think more positively and overcome self-sabotage?

2. How do I adopt good habits, act quicker and make better decisions?

3. How do I use discipline to avoid procrastination and perfectionism?

4. How do I focus better, live in the moment, and listen to what people say?

5. How do I learn faster and improve my memory, especially as I get older?

6. What is lucid dreaming and how can I use it to better solve problems?

7. How do I reduce my anxiety, increase my confidence and become more self-sufficient?

This order makes a lot of sense to me. Positivity is an easy win, which leads into habits. Use habits long-term to achieve discipline, and implement that discipline to get focused. Then, the three advanced chapters at the end: memory, lucid dreaming, confidence.

Next, map out your chapters by listing **Why**, **What**, **How-To**, and **What-If** sub-questions. Optionally, add three keywords next to each sub-question to give you a prompt to help you answer. I won't flesh out the entire outline, but I'll flesh out one single 8-minute, 1200 word, 4-to-6 page chapter:

How can I find my life purpose, get excited, avoid boredom, think more positively and overcome self-sabotage?

- **Why** is a life purpose and goals so important? (busyness, meaning, 80/20)

- **What** are the reasons many people are happy, unhappy, bored or fulfilled? (comparison, no gratitude, comfort zone)

- **How** do I begin to make a change if I am not where I want to be in life, what are the steps? (inventory, journaling, visualization)

- Once I've course-corrected my trajectory in life, **what** new possibilities are available to me? (time, passion not dependent on money, connection)

To help you understand this process, I'll also build out the "memory" chapter:

- Title: "How do I learn faster and improve my memory, especially as I get older?"

- **Why** is a good memory so important? (less stress, better career, thoughtful to others

- **What** tools will help me strengthen my memory? (mnemonic devices, studying, sleep)

- **How** can I improve memory, what are some exercises I can perform? (walk, read out loud, sticky notes)

- **What if** I improve my memory, what benefits will I enjoy? (organized, healthy, less risk of dementia/depression)

Anytime I've found myself stuck when creating a book --
whether that's staring at a blank page or feeling like I have
half a book and a little bit of a sunk-cost problem, I fall back
on the formula:

- Ask a single question that my entire book solves

- Research on Google, YouTube and Amazon to see
  what 10 sub-questions break down the main problem

- Reduce those ten questions down to seven

- Re-arrange into a logical order that makes sense:
  usually four simple questions and three advanced
  ones

- Build out each sub-question into four sub-sub-
  questions each: **Why, What, How-To, and What-If**

- Use Zencastr.com and my computer's built-in
  microphone (or a Blue Yeti) to speak out each sub-
  sub-question in the outline, plus each two-minute
  answer. The end-result is a 56-minute recording
  asking one big question, seven sub-questions, and
  four sub-sub-questions within each

- Send the recording to Rev.com for transcription

- Clean up that written transcription through several
  editing passes

- Format the book with chapter headings, page numbers, table of contents, hyperlinks, images, and legal pages (such as a Disclaimer and About the Author page)

- Hire a book cover from Fiverr.com

- Login to KDP.Amazon.com, fill in the form to define title, pricing, etc. Submit the book cover graphic, and the Word doc (interior or manuscript)

That's how you create a book. Not by winging it, and not by overthinking it. By relying on a proven formula and then applying your structured creativity within those bounds.

Explaining the book process is one thing, but would you like to see it in action? Our course that shows how to create your book in a day, a week, or any time frame that is convenient for you -- is available at MakeAProduct.com.

I'm hoping you're beginning to see that WWHW (**Why, What, How-To, What-If**) appears everywhere, and you can use it to solve almost any problem -- especially that "pesky" problem of speaking or writing.

Chapter 8: WWHW for *Videos, Podcasts & Courses*

Do you have any excuse to be starved for content ever again? Writer's block? Speaking into a camera? Explaining a process to someone? Only if you intentionally self-sabotage.

When all else fails, fall back onto the **Why**, **What**, **How-To**, **What-If** formula to buy yourself some time.

I first stumbled upon this concept when YouTube was fairly new and so was content marketing. I wanted to click the record button and speak on-the-spot, but I found myself getting stuck halfway, or worse, wondering if I'd rambled on for too long without a coherent point.

The crude solution at the time was to think of three letters — **the rule of threes**. This was my thought process:

I'm recording a video explaining how to take massive imperfect action. I'll think of three sub-topics...

- **Sub-Topic #1:** Set milestones instead of 5-year goals (letter M for Milestones)

- **Sub-Topic #2:** Take some amount of action every day even if it's only five minutes (letter A for Actions)

- **Sub-Topic #3:** Get the results of those actions to a shippable or completed stage as fast as possible (C for Completed)

- I'd only have to remember the letters **M-A-C** to cue myself about those three points

That simple technique alone helped me to be more well-spoken, but I found myself falling into the trap I mentioned earlier of simply "speaking out a list." No context, no emotions, no relatability, no fun. Only the facts. Although using three letters to represent three talking points was fun, I later realized that WWHW was far superior, and those M-A-C three points belonged in the **How-To** or "problem-solving" section of my video.

A better structure:

- **Why** is it so important to take massive imperfect action? Can I relate to burnout, disappointment from lack of results, or the guilt from not doing enough?

- **What** key components should be in place that most people are missing, such as accountability, deadlines, and a quiet focused location?

- **How** do Milestones, daily Actions, and Completion help me take consistent action?

- **What if** I take consistent action, what next step should I take, or even better, what website address should I visit in order to get more information?

The above is fleshed out just enough to deliver something impactful in a short amount of time, and it is a formula you will begin to see everywhere in your daily life.

Example: You hear an ad on the radio while you're driving. Whether it's an advertisement for MyPillow, Motel 6, or a weight loss system, it's positioned as WWHW: **Why** should I listen to this message (the Attention-getter)? **What** problem are you setting up (Interest-builder)? **How** will you solve it (Desire)? **What-If** I take the action of visiting that website or calling a phone number (Action)?

I use the WWHW formula every time I record an iTunes Apple Podcast (online radio show) episode -- I begin with the problem that led the person to listen to that episode, I explain the **What** (concepts to catch the person up and give context), and then dive into **How-To** solve that problem. I end with the **What-If** section... after getting this information, what are the next steps? What website should you visit to get more information?

Online Courses

I get most of my traffic from podcasting, but I make most of my money from digital online courses (membership sites). You may know someone who has earned an online degree, or perhaps learned something from a website such as uDemy or Lynda. If you have the ability to teach just one person about weight loss, real estate, the stock market, etc. (to get your own piece of the "digital course" pie) you may have become intrigued about the possibilities of teaching once and getting paid again and again, but were discouraged about the finer details.

This may be too technical, but here's the process I fall back on when creating a course that solves a problem:

- What **problem** does my course solve? What is the end result? What tangible thing will my student have created? Not just learned, but created, within 30 days?

- What are the four "milestones" **(modules or lessons)** that get someone from Point A (having nothing) to Point B (results: lost weight, renting a home, etc.) one week at a time?

- My template for those **four weekly modules** adding up to a 30-day course: week 1 (deliver a quick win), week 2 (deliver the exciting result they want), week 3 (sneak in what they really need), week 4 (case studies and loose ends)

- When planning a 60- to 90 minute-module, I use **Why, What, How-To, What-If** to plan: **Why** are we here? What problem will we solve? **What** steps will we take to solve the problem? Then, **How-To** solve that problem, in step-by-step detail? Finally, **What-If** you apply that material? What's a quick homework assignment or challenge gets that you started?

I apologize if the above goes over your head, but if you're interested in creating an online course and you'd rather get it done using a template instead of becoming a perfectionist, visit MembershipCube.com to see what that's all about.

Conclusion: *Who & Where*

I have an honest question for you: "Who" Cares?

Does anyone care how many hours you put into creating your website, how many impressive degrees you have, or how many years you've been in business? Do they care about your logo? Probably not!

Two final questions to ponder as you refine your message and promote your cause: **Who** are the people you want to talk to, and **Where** are they?

Consider the YouTube channel filled with hundreds of videos that show: zero views, zero views, zero views...

Versus the person who hangs out on forums and Facebook Groups, or networks in offline masterminds. Listens to what people say and delivers a solution.

It's easy to fall into the trap of "Keeping Up with the Joneses." You have that competitor who gets under your skin because they seem to have their marketing dialed in. A beautiful website and established social media presence. Paid ads that follow you around the internet!

Instead of simply cloning, one-upping, me-too-ing, and drawing attention to THEM, do this: become a customer of that competitor. Use their training or their software, not for the express purposes of copying, but to find the flaw.

Blue Ocean Strategy

Discover where it falls short, get frustrated and create a BETTER (perhaps even unrelated, paradigm shifting, non-competing) solution.

The problem with following your competitors is that you compete in what's called a "red ocean" (as explained by W. Chan Kim) -- it's crowded and cutthroat with already-established rules. It's better to create something new in a "blue ocean" where there is more opportunity and less competition. Think about how revolutionary Uber was compared to taxis, or how the iPad was marketed as a simpler alternative to laptops.

I began my career in an industry where the average person marketed a $7 e-book that taught others how to make money selling $7 e-books. Instead of being like everyone else, I created and sold web page creation software, templates, and tools for that crowd of people to setup websites, membership sites, and podcasts.

Another niche we market to: voiceover artists. People who have been "passed over" by the voice-acting "Establishment" and want to generate their own income by using freelancer sites (Fiverr, Upwork, Audible) to work their own hours. Meanwhile, those still competing in the "red ocean" are voiceover artists not making money, trying to sell coaching services to other voiceover artists not making money.

One of our favorite clients, Dr. Charles Runels, invented a PRP (platelet rich plasma) procedure called the Vampire Facelift, a new way to restore color and youthful appearance to one's face. He markets this procedure to other doctors to provide a needed high-ticket service and help them escape the "rat race" of struggling to run a medical practice.

I mention these examples to you to tell you to decide **Who** you are speaking to, and **Where** they hang out. If your podcast episodes drone on for too long with no real point, or you're stuck with "writer's block" -- then chances are, you aren't writing to a person. Your **Who** does not exist. You're trying to please everyone. It isn't clear if you're showing off to your competitors (bad) or your prospects (good).

Communicate to One Person

Early on, I struggled with writing. It took me weeks to crank out one single email to promote my business, I wasn't building a list, and it took months to create a short article or blog post.

I practiced (repeated) until I strengthened by writing muscle and I applied the WWHW formula in order to write quickly. Writing quickly added enthusiasm and allowed me to crank out content on a massive scale. This evolved into my habit of broadcasting to my email list every day. When I contacted my subscribers daily, I made more money -- imagine that!

However, I lacked traffic. I partnered with Lance Tamashiro from Lehi, Utah (just outside of Salt Lake City) who I consider to be the smartest internet marketer on the planet.

Lance's wife Martie visited my websites and subscribed to my email subscriber list to find out what this strange redheaded guy Robert Plank from Turlock, California (two hours East of San Francisco) was all about.

One day, Lance noticed his wife sitting at the laptop, deeply focused, rapidly typing a message. He asked, "What are you writing?" Her response: "Your new business partner Robert emailed me and I'm replying."

Lance looked at the screen. It was a broadcast email that I had sent to 40,000+ subscribers (it even had an unsubscribe link at the bottom) but Martie thought the message had been sent directly to her -- because I keep ONE person in mind (with a specific need) when writing.

Don't worry about a niche. Don't concern yourself with multiple "customer avatars" if that thinking only complicates things. Don't think about how much time, work, writing, proofreading, editing, and re-working you'll have to do. Instead, keep that *person* in mind. The best kind of writing, speaking, or video creation you'll ever create is a letter to an old friend that helps solve their problem in an easy and timely fashion. That's it!

Today, everything can be edited or corrected later, AND you are expected to move quickly. Think about how the average person gets tired of their phone just because it's "last year's model." Use WWHW (**Why, What, How-To, What-If**) to create content quickly, get your message out there, see what resonates, and adjust.

People talk about a red ocean and a blue ocean as if it's a one-time event. You may currently live in a red ocean, move to the blue ocean to plant your flag, and readjust in a year or two if your blue ocean becomes too crowded. Eugene Schwartz refers to this as **Five Levels of Awareness:**

- Unaware (stories & secrets)

- Problem Aware (benefits & anxieties)

- Solution Aware (claims & proof)

- Product Aware (discounts & deals)

- Most Aware (product & price)

Your marketplace travels through the phases of:

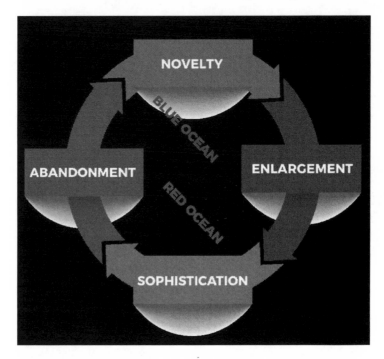

- **Novelty** (you're in a completely blue ocean and have no competitors)

- **Enlargement** (competitors out-do each other being bigger & better)

- **Sophistication** (piling on features, speed, convenience)

- **Abandonment** (the marketplace becomes a crowded red ocean, consumers become jaded, it's time to market based on emotions and possibly find a new blue ocean)

The point I'm trying to make with all this is:

- Stop thinking. **Start doing.** Rely on a formula to eliminate decision-making and thinking in your communicating/writing/speaking.

- **It's easier to edit crap than air.** Don't edit as you go. Instead, get the idea in a concrete form in its simplest form, then refine it later.

- Set **goals (with deadlines)** that excite you and get you focused on the end-goal, not on the "work."

- Think about **the person you're helping solve a problem** to avoid thinking about your faults/insecurities.

- Move fast enough that you can put yourself out of business, replacing it with a new business.

"Creativity is intelligence having fun."
-- Albert Einstein

"Failure is the opportunity to begin again more intelligently."
-- Henry Ford

"We would worry less about what others think of us if we realized how seldom they do."
-- Ethel Barrett

If you'd like to stay in touch and stay up-to-date about the latest marketing trends and techniques, you'll want to subscribe to my podcast at <u>MarketerOfTheDay.com</u>. If the formulas and templates we've discussed in this book sound interesting (content marketing, video creation, blogging, writing a book, podcasting, or membership sites) and you'd like to have a discussion about how to implement, contact me at <u>RobertPlank.com/contact</u>.

If you've experienced an "ah-ha" (mindset shift) at any point in your life, you were never able to see the world the same ever again. The mind, once expanded, can never return to its previous contracted state. It is my sincere hope that, from now on, you see WWHW (**Why, What, How-To, What-If**) everywhere you go, and that you use it to communicate effectively.

About the Author

Robert Plank is an online business coach who would like to help you manage your time, get your life back, and simplify your daily activities.

Using systems, checklists, and templates, you can write a book within an hour and become a published author in 12 hours. You can setup a membership site in one day, create a blog or podcast in 5 minutes or less, and so much more.

- Podcast: MarketerOfTheDay.com

- Bonus Materials: WWHWBook.com

Leave a Quick Review

If you enjoyed (or hated) this book, want to give feedback or tell others what you thought of it, I'd be eternally grateful if you could give me your honest opinion at:

WWHWBook.com/amazon

Suggestions about what to post in your review:

- **Quick Sentence #1 (Why):** What problem did you have that led you to searching or finding the WWHW book?
- **Quick Sentence #2 (What):** What one thing interested you about this book? What caught your attention?
- **Quick Sentence #3 (How):** How did this book help solve your problem, or what solution did you learn that will help you moving forward?
- **Quick Sentence #4 (What-If):** What's one good reason someone reading your review would want this book?

I look forward to hearing your thoughts.

Made in the USA
San Bernardino, CA
28 January 2020